ALASKA

Karen Durrie

www.av2books.com

LET'S READ
AV²
BY WEIGL™
ADDED VALUE • AUDIO VISUAL

Go to **www.av2books.com,** and enter this book's unique code.

BOOK CODE

C132465

AV² by Weigl brings you media enhanced books that support active learning.

AV² provides enriched content that supplements and complements this book. Weigl's AV² books strive to create inspired learning and engage young minds in a total learning experience.

Your AV² Media Enhanced books come alive with...

Audio
Listen to sections of the book read aloud.

Video
Watch informative video clips.

Embedded Weblinks
Gain additional information for research.

Try This!
Complete activities and hands-on experiments.

Key Words
Study vocabulary, and complete a matching word activity.

Quizzes
Test your knowledge.

Slide Show
View images and captions, and prepare a presentation.

... and much, much more!

Published by AV² by Weigl
350 5th Avenue, 59th Floor
New York, NY 10118
Website: www.av2books.com   www.weigl.com

Library of Congress Cataloging-in-Publication Data

Durrie, Karen.
 Alaska / Karen Durrie.
   p. cm. -- (Explore the U.S.A.)
 Includes bibliographical references and index.
 ISBN 978-1-61913-323-5 (hard cover : alk. paper)
 1. Alaska--Juvenile literature. I. Title.
 F904.3.D87 2012
 979.8--dc23
                         2012014754

Printed in the United States of America in North Mankato, Minnesota
1 2 3 4 5 6 7 8 9 16 15 14 13 12

052012
WEP040512

Project Coordinator: Karen Durrie
Art Director: Terry Paulhus

Weigl acknowledges Getty Images as the primary image supplier for this title.

2

ALASKA

Contents

This is Alaska.
It is called The Last Frontier.
Alaska is farther north than
any other state.

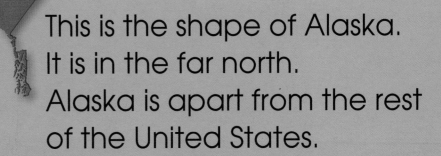

This is the shape of Alaska.
It is in the far north.
Alaska is apart from the rest
of the United States.

Where is Alaska?

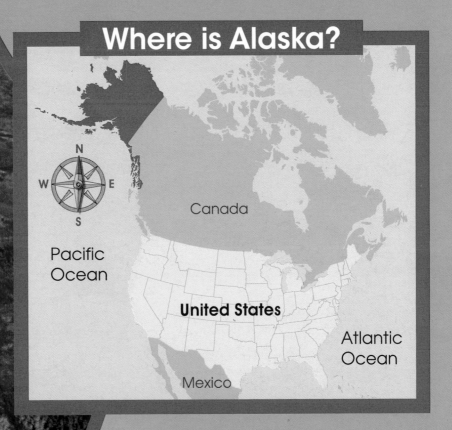

N
W E
S

Pacific
Ocean

Canada

United States

Atlantic
Ocean

Mexico

Alaska borders Canada.

People went to Alaska to find gold. This time in history was called the Gold Rush.

More than 100,000 people looked for gold during the Gold Rush.

The forget-me-not is the Alaska state flower. Forget-me-nots can grow in rocky places.

The state seal has mountains, a ship, and the northern lights.

THE SEAL OF THE STATE OF ALASKA

The northern lights make the night sky glow red, green, yellow, and blue.

This is the state flag of Alaska. It is blue with eight yellow stars.

Seven stars make the Big Dipper at the bottom. The North Star is at the top.

The state animal of Alaska is the moose. About 200,000 moose live in Alaska. One moose can weigh up to 1,600 pounds.

Alaska has the largest moose on Earth.

This is the capital city of Alaska. It is named Juneau. More than 20,000 bald eagles live around Juneau.

People can only get to Juneau by air or sea.

MOOSE LODGE

PATRIOT

17

Oil is found in Alaska. A big pipe takes oil across the state. Ships take the oil to places where it is made into fuel.

More than 672 billion gallons of oil have moved through this pipe.

The Alaska state sport is dog mushing. People race on sleds pulled by dogs.

Alaska has the most famous sled dog race in the world.

ALASKA FACTS

These pages provide detailed information that expands on the interesting facts found in the book. These pages are intended to be used by adults as a learning support to help young readers round out their knowledge of each state in the *Explore the U.S.A.* series.

Pages 4–5

Alaska is called The Last Frontier because of its distance from the lower 48 states and for its rugged geography. Alaska is also called the Land of the Midnight Sun. During summer, there are parts of Alaska that do not get dark at night. Towns close to the Arctic Circle experience a polar day, where the Sun stays in the sky for 24 hours.

Pages 6–7

On January 3, 1959, Alaska became the 49th state to join the United States. Russia owned Alaska before the United States bought it for $7.2 million in 1867. Alaska covers 590,693 square miles (1, 529,888 square kilometers). This is more than twice the size of Texas. Despite its size, only about 710,000 people live in Alaska, making it the third smallest state in population.

Pages 8–9

Gold was discovered in Alaska many years before the Klondike Gold Rush. However, when a large strike was made in Canada near the Alaska border, one of the biggest gold rushes in history began. More than 100,000 people went north to the Yukon and Alaska to seek their fortunes. The gold rush took place between 1896 and 1900.

Pages 10–11

The forget-me-not flower grows all over Alaska. It has no scent during the day, but it is fragrant at night. The state seal was designed in 1910, while Alaska was still a territory. The symbols on the seal represent important industries and resources in Alaska, such as fishing, mining, railroads, forests, and sea transportation.

The Alaska flag was designed in 1927 by a 13-year-old boy named Benny Benson. He submitted his design into a contest and won. The blue of the Alaska flag represents the Alaska sky and the forget-me-not flower. The Big Dipper is part of Ursa Major constellation, which forms the image of a bear. This animal is found throughout Alaska. The North Star refers to Alaska's position as the northernmost state.

The Alaska-Yukon moose is the largest member of the deer family. Only male moose, or bulls, have antlers. Moose shed and regrow their antlers each year. Moose antlers grow very large when the animal reaches about 10 years old. A bull moose can add 1 pound (0.5 kilograms) and 1 inch (2.5 centimeters) of antler bone per day in the summer.

Juneau was officially founded in 1880 by prospectors Joe Juneau and Richard Harris, who discovered gold in a creek there. People must travel to Juneau by boat or plane. There is no road connecting Juneau to the rest of Alaska. Roads in the area are difficult to build on the terrain and hard to maintain because of frequent avalanches.

The Trans-Alaska Pipeline System carries oil 800 miles (1,287 kilometers) to the port city of Valdez. Construction on the pipeline began in 1975 and was completed in 1977. Oil tankers transport oil to refineries to be made into various fuels and substances used to make goods. Since 1959, Alaska has made more than $157 billion from its oil.

Dog mushing is a sport in which teams of dogs pull sleds over snow. The musher, or sled driver, rides on the sled. People come from around the world to watch the Iditarod dogsled race. The race covers 1,150 miles (1,851 km) and takes 9 to 12 days to complete. The winner of the race receives money and a new truck.

KEY WORDS

Research has shown that as much as 65 percent of all written material published in English is made up of 300 words. These 300 words cannot be taught using pictures or learned by sounding them out. They must be recognized by sight. This book contains 59 common sight words to help young readers improve their reading fluency and comprehension. This book also teaches young readers several important content words, such as proper nouns. These words are paired with pictures to aid in learning and improve understanding.

Page	Sight Words First Appearance
4	any, it, is, last, other, state, than, the, this
7	far, from, in, of, where
8	find, for, more, people, time, to, was, went
11	a, and, can, grow, has, make, mountains, night, places
12	at, with
15	about, animal, Earth, live, on, one, up
16	air, around, by, city, get, named, only, or, sea
19	big, found, have, into, made, moved, takes, through
20	most, world

Page	Content Words First Appearance
4	Alaska, frontier
7	Canada, north, shape, United States
8	gold, Gold Rush, history
11	flower, forget-me-not, northern lights, seal, ship, sky
12	Big Dipper, bottom, flag, North Star, stars, top
15	moose, pounds
16	bald eagles, Juneau
19	fuel, gallons, oil, pipe
20	dog mushing, dogs, race, sleds, sport

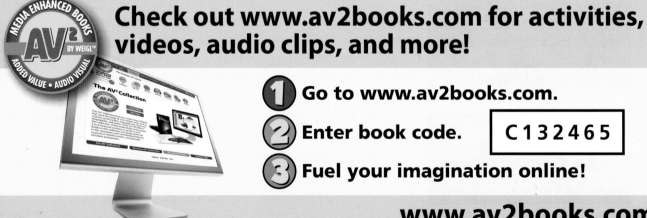

Check out www.av2books.com for activities, videos, audio clips, and more!

1 Go to www.av2books.com.

2 Enter book code. C 1 3 2 4 6 5

3 Fuel your imagination online!

www.av2books.com